AMAZING SPOT WHAT!

Nick Bryant & Rowan Summers

HINKLER BOOKS

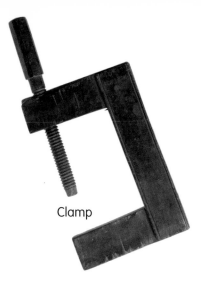

Clamp

Cog

Cat

Also available in this series:

Spot What Picture Hunt
Spot What Magical
Spot What Spectacular

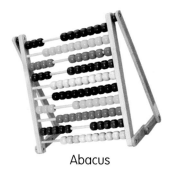

Abacus

First published in 2002 by Hinkler Books Pty Ltd
17 - 23 Redwood Drive, Dingley, Vic, 3172, Australia.

HB
HINKLER
BOOKS

© Hinkler Books Pty Ltd 2002

10
08 10 09 07
ISBN: 1865157279

Joker

Car

Printed and bound in China

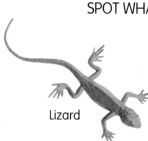

Lizard

Mouse

Contents

Balloon

Knight

Whistle

Vice

Can you spot a
Duck and a bat,
A blimp, a squid
And three different hats,

A witch, a kite,
A pie in the sky,
Three parachutes
And a pig that can fly?

There's a boomerang,
A lost umbrella,
Six balloons and
A purple propeller.

FINAL FRONTIER

SPOT WHAT

SPACE RACE FINISH LINE

WELCOME TO CYBERSPACE

FIZZO

Can you spot a magnet, a CD and TV,
A sailing ship, a house and a chimpanzee,
A barrel, a bottle and four starfish,
Five astronauts and a satellite dish?
Find a golf ball and a horse with wings,
A nut, a bolt and planetary rings.

Can you spot an apple core,
A bunch of grapes, a soda can,
Corn on the cob and two hot dogs,
A carrot and a gingerbread man?

Can you find a pizza pie,
Three different types of cheese,
An avocado, half a tomato,
And four little honey bees?

Can you spot a pair of pliers,
An axe, a vice, three colored wires,
A hard hat and some plans on paper,
A dripping tap and a scraping scraper?
Find a torch, two springs and two locks,
Three paint splats and a red toolbox.

Can you spot a leopard,
A cow, two bulls, two seals,
Two stone cats, a welcome mat,
And three ferris wheels?

Can you find a baby bear,
A vintage car, a spear,
Five dinosaurs, a clock, a score,
A moose, a sheep, a deer?

AMAZING FALLS ->

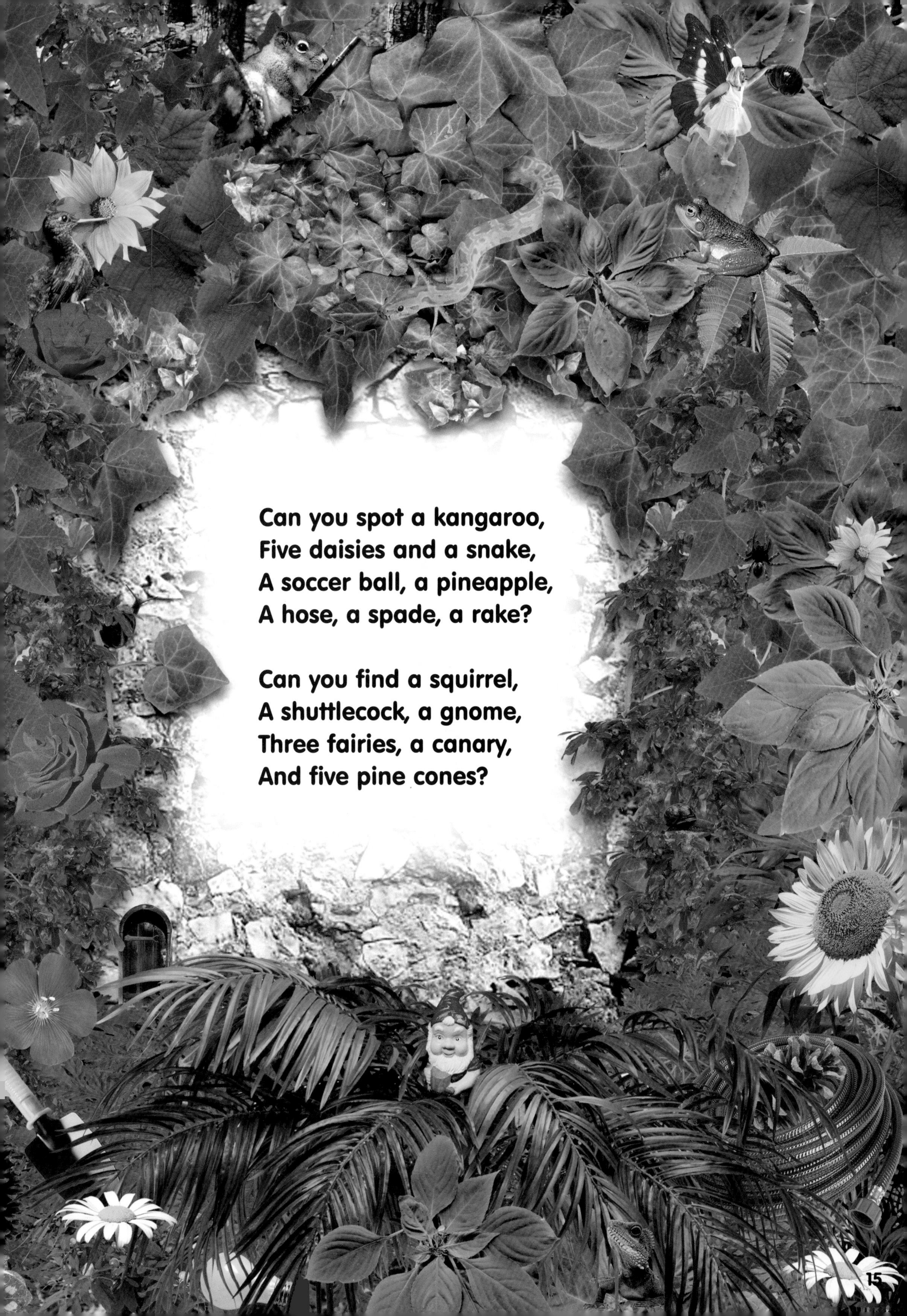

Can you spot a kangaroo,
Five daisies and a snake,
A soccer ball, a pineapple,
A hose, a spade, a rake?

Can you find a squirrel,
A shuttlecock, a gnome,
Three fairies, a canary,
And five pine cones?

SPOT WHAT 2

MEOW

16

Can you spot a bird and a pen,
A telephone and ten past ten,
A truck, a puppet, two buckets, a tie,
A rabbit, a boot and a butterfly?
Find a juke box, a feather, a star,
A whistle, a flipper, a drum and guitar.

8 + 1 = ?

11-9=2

2 + 3 = 5

15

12 - 7 =

6 + 5 =

$8 \times 7 = 56$

Can you spot a measuring tape,
And a bright red bus,
A computer and the pyramids,
Three coins, an abacus?

Can you find nine rabbits,
Two sums that total seven,
A crane, a train, an hour glass,
Three sums that equal eleven?

8-3=5

5+1=6

1+1=2

1+11=12

AMAZING

?=4

3x5=15

6 - 2 = ?

5 + 2 =

```
        00181
62)11222
        62
        502
        ?96
         62
         62
          0
```

1969 396 05E

2215

Can you spot a set of keys,
And a red lipstick,
Seven coins, a pack of gum,
And a little candlestick?

Can you spot three brushes,
And a sticky first-aid strip,
Golden wings, five shiny rings,
And a tiny pair of lips?

To you with love

Can you spot three dominos,
Two giraffes and tic-tac-toe,
Three red dice, another blue,
A pawn, a knight and a joker too?
Find eight jacks, a queen, a king,
Two darts, a clown and a yo-yo string.

FISHMONGERS

Next Millennium's Forecast
Strong solar winds
Expected high 5000 degrees
Nighttime low 0 (Absolute Zero)

WEATHER

test signal - please standby -

Spot
Noodle

NEW
EARWAX
FLAVOR

SNEW

Can you spot a goldfish,
An apple and cartoon,
A skier, wolf and tomahawk,
A spider and baboon?

Find a bear, a skunk, a poodle,
And a slide trombone,
A donkey and a lobster,
A watch and microphone.

NEWS
SPOT
WHAT!
17

NEW
WOR
PEA

Can you spot a pumpkin head,
Three balls and a dragon,
Two lizards and a wizard,
And a little red wagon?

Can you find a pair of gloves,
Two orange boots and a frog,
A car, a train, a cowboy,
Three mice, two cats, four dogs?

AMAZING

See if you can spot these things in every picture:

Can you find the words 'SPOT WHAT,'
A mermaid and a four,
A ladybug, a lightbulb,
And a little blue door?

Juke Box

Kazoo

Blimp

Rules For The Spot What Amazing Game

1. Flip a coin, to see who goes first.
2. The winner of the coin toss chooses a picture from the book and then picks something for the other person to find, saying, for example, 'Can you spot a pumpkin head?'
3. The spotter must then find the item.
4. If he or she can't spot it, the winner gets 5 points and shows him or her where it is.

5. Then the winner takes another turn and chooses an item for the other person to spot.
6. If the spotter can find the item, then he or she gets 5 points and now it's his or her turn.
7. The first to reach 30 points wins but you could also set your own limit of 50, or even 100 points.

You can also make the game more interesting by putting a time limit of one to three minutes on the search.

Solitaire Game

Jack

The Spot What Challenge

The following items are much harder to find, so get ready for the challenge.

Scraper

King

Flight
(page 4/5)

A butterfly
4 green leaves
3 hour glasses
An eagle
The world's first plane
A pair of socks
2 elastic bands

Food
(page 8/9)

3 balloons
3 chilli peppers
Some teeth
A Christmas tree
6 peanuts
6 blue candles
6 strawberries

Cat

Space
(page 6/7)

All 12 zodiac symbols
A parking meter
A picnic
A space shuttle
4 telescopes
Venus and Mars
A kazoo

Tools
(page 10/11)

5 keys
A needle
3 cogs
3 measuring tools
3 different saws
A microscope
A metronome

Boomerang

Ferris Wheel

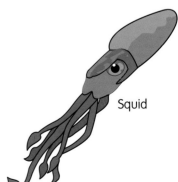
Squid

Tomahawk

Soda Can

Arena
(page 12/13)

7 jacks
5 barrels
An indian brave
A moon
4 shields
The words "GO GO DANCE"
A path to spell AMAZING

Blue
(page 16/17)

A typewriter
A seahorse
12 musical notes
5 fish
4 boats
4 balls
A rocking chair

Mermaid

Nature
(page 14/15)

A spider
An owl
A hungry bee
A nest
2 lizards
7 snails
A hummingbird

Numbers
(Page 18/19)

The word "APRIL"
2 boats
3 dominos
A barometer
4 playing cards
The word "RADAR"
The Sun

Metronome

World's First Plane

Spade

Zodiac Symbol

Purse
(page 20/21)

5 diamonds
A frog
A cat
A pair of scissors
An umbrella
A ticket to Wonderland
A pen

Monitors
(page 24/25)

7 escaped butterflies
A potted plant
A rock band
A door handle
A jack
2 cameras
"CHANNEL 17"

Egg With Legs

Games
(page 22/23)

A fish bowl
A dog
4 flies
A thimble
Solitaire game
A pig
14 marbles

Bedroom
(page 26/27)

4 dinosaurs
23 yellow stars
An elephant
6 musical instruments
A fairy
A green plane
7 bears

Dog

Cowboy

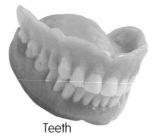
Teeth

Hourglass

Acknowledgements

We would like to thank the following people:

Albert Meli from Continuous Recall
Sam Grimmer
Peter Wakeman
Peter Tovey Studios
Samantha Boardman
Kelly-Anne Thompson
Kristie Maxwell
Kate Bryant
Heather Hammonds
Miles Summers
Little Ashlie, Michael, Nicole and James for lending their toys

Special thanks to Tsutomu Higo for the use of geometric models for 'Numbers'
www.asahi-net.or.jp/~nj2t-hg/

Furniture for 'Bedroom' created by:
Christopher Peregrine Timms
www.christophertimms.com.au

Barometer

Shuttlecock

Diamond